Tilly The Turtle

ISBN: 9 781471 698583

Tilly The Turtle

Isabel Scheck

This book belongs to :

___ ___ ___ ___ ___ ___

___ ___ ___ ___ ___ ___

This is Tilly Turtle
and Mummy Turtle and
they love to swim together
in the deep blue sea.

One day Mummy and Tilly went off together,
Tilly swam away when she saw a pretty shell.
It was very shiny!

②

Then, when she looked around, Tilly couldn't find her Mummy. This made her sad and called out "Mummy, where are you?"

She got no answer, but she saw that someone was waiting for her.

It was Sharky the shark who came to say hello!
Tilly asked him:

Have you seen my Mummy?

No I haven't. I'm sorry!
I hope you find her though!

Hmm. Maybe Annie knows...

Tilly The Turtle went off to find out if Annie the Anglerfish knew where her Mummy was. Annie did not, so Tilly said her goodbyes and swam off to find her.

⑤

Next, Tilly met Jimmy
the Jellyfish.
"Have you seen my
Mummy?"

"No I haven't, but I
think I know who has!
Try Sara the Seal.

Tilly said, "thank you."
She was still a bit sad, but she felt better
when she talked to her friends.

"Have you seen my Mummy?"

Sara the Seal also hadn't seen Mummy Turtle, but she told Tilly that Sophie the Stingray was waiting to help her.

Can you see her too?

7

"Hi Tilly!
I heard from
Jimmy the Jellyfish
that you're were
looking for your Mummy,
is that right?"

When she said yes, Sophie suggested that the turtle climb on her back so they could swim around the sea together to have a look.

⑧

Tilly The Turtle and Sophie The Stingray continued swimming together. Tilly felt better now that the stingray was with her.

9

When they'd been swimming and talking for a long time, Tilly and Sophie met Suzy The Seahorse. She also didn't know where Mummy Turtle was.

"Don't worry, Tilly," said Sophie The Stingray, "we'll find her!"

10

"Hi Oscar, have you seen my Mummy?"
Tilly asked Oscar The Octopus.
"No, sorry, but I think Ellie The Eel knows!"
Sophie and Tilly said thank you and went
off to find Ellie the Eel... Can you find her?

Tilly The Turtle enjoyed riding on Sophie as they swam. She even fell asleep as the stingray talked to Ellie The Eel. Ellie wanted to go with her friends and so, she did.

12

When Tilly woke up she asked Star The Starfish, "Have you seen my Mummy?

"No, I'm sorry, I haven't, but I hope you find her," said Star, "but maybe Lily The Lump fish knows?"

Once Star had told them where Lily was, Tilly said thank you and bye bye.

⑬

Tilly and Mummy were so happy and
they hugged each other.
Sophie The Stingray and Lily The
Lump Fish were also happy to see
them together again.

Then, Mummy, Tilly and her friends all played together.

16

Abot the Author

Isabel comes from England, but lives in Switzerland with her parents and her brother. She works with children, which she adores, but she also loves to write; especially in the genres of fantasy, poetry and romance. She uses experiences and images as inspiration to create words. Isabel also loves to express herself by drawing.

When she's not writing you can find her on Twitter at @Izzy597 or Instagram at @Isabelscheck97.